Gold Light Shining

Gold Light Shining

Bebe Ashley

BANSHEE
PRESS

First published 2020 by
Banshee Press
www.bansheelit.com

A CIP record for this title is available from the British Library.

Banshee Press gratefully acknowledges
the financial assistance of the Arts Council.

ISBN: 978-0-9956550-8-9

Set in Palatino by Eimear Ryan
Cover design by Anna Morrison
Printed in Ireland by Walsh Colour Print

Everyone in that room is on the same page
and everyone knows what I stand for.
I'm not saying I understand how it feels.
I'm just trying to say, 'I see you'.
– HARRY STYLES

Harry,
I'm not saying I understand how it feels.
I'm just trying to say, 'I see you'.

Contents

Fandom

Fangirl

Fanfic

Fan Mail

Gold Light Shining

Fandom

Kiwi / Kiwi / Kiwi

The boy with the Gucci guitar strings
is playing glam rock to a room of strangers.

His photographer captures a group of girls in knock-
off floral suits and pink sequin Chelsea boots.

Hearts thumping heaving jumping, his final song
shakes the sweat-slick stage on the concrete floor.

The guitarist who used to work in the pizza shop
looks to the bassist, the keys, the drummer

to know if this is normal. It is not normal:
people are having the time of their lives.

Never Going Back Now

Nobody knew I would spend the next year
writing about flares with flora and fauna print.

I think most about the yellow silk trousers,
their shelves of potted plants climbing the inseam.

Nearly always a continent away, I wait
in the wrong time zone for lights up,

for pixels of dry ice and smoke to clear
in the poor connection of the periscope.

It wasn't until the embellishments of Basel
that I started preparing for next year's silhouette.

With a travel scholarship, with *Beauty Papers*,
I elaborate on a Peter Pan collar and pearls.

Carolina

In the photograph on the fridge we had just met.
She was wonderful but I was dizzy with jetlag
so there is a blur to the moment of capture.
It was New Year's Eve and we waited
for the fright of fireworks to wake us.
She laughed behind her spoon as I stirred
half a teaspoon of honey through her coffee,
a miniature of sloe gin into my own.
It was only when she was distracted
by three glass ramekins of coconut cake
that I found the right aperture.
I haven't seen her since but I remember her name
and what her grandmother texted at the turn of the year.

(Pretty) Woman

Before the wind blows you away, I want you
to know I haven't slept in four nights,

but in the attic I watched three thousand
tiny white lights ebb and swell.

Behind the patterns of the marble tub,
let's strip to bubble-gum silk –

Champagne is burning a hole
in the pocket of your dressing gown.

Ever Since New York

I've kept my head down, darling.
Started swimming early enough
that the night porter waves me in.

Waves me out so that the freezing fog
will crystallize loose strands of hair
falling from my half-up half-down elastic.

The insomniac at the bagel stand salutes me.
Green tea. Gravlax, cream cheese
topped with a few drops of lemon.

There are flashing lights already
and the bookshop is slow to open.
I pretend to know everything while I wait.

On Church Avenue I light candles,
like the way the flame burns for
the quickest moment under my thumb.

Adored

The ice-cream van stalls by the sea wall.
On a day like this, the beach would be empty
if the wind-breaker-litter-picker hadn't noticed

the boy plucking pebbles from the rock pools
who slips the heaviest stones into his pockets,
who is somewhat smiling as a crumbling flake is pushed

into the soft serve and held out from the sandbar.
Only for him to wave it off, with a grazed palm still oozing,
still stinging salt, from a splintered obsidian shell.

The crabs scuttle sideways into the seaweed.
The bell of the jellyfish blooms towards his fingertips.
His pockets drip and drip as he walks into the sea.

Sweet Creature

It is impossible to watch you kiss a strawberry
from a polite distance.

Nobody seems to dance well in Venice but you
and you are not even well.

The marble here swallows the wolves
and their whores obedient and abused.

Our black night is humbled by the chaos
that is salt and ice intermingled.

Take heaven, I'll steal the soft parts of hell for you
drowsy on syrups of the world.

Go, leave me in the garden of the castle
I am almost happily on my knees.

Meet Me in the Hallway

It is Sunday at the art gallery, but I cannot look at the art.
There is a plug socket and an on / off switch on the wall.
I catch a myriad of blues and purples from NIGHT, TANGIER.
Not dissimilar to the colours I left around my wrist,
because it was time to meet new people and the girls here
hug each other, but do not know me well enough to ask permission.
I am equidistant from two exit signs. The first the better choice
in a swooping staircase under skylight. The second leads past
the catalogue translations, the water fountain, families.
Nobody had held me by my elbow before. I shiver.
Wishing I had morphine to dull the flicker of neon green
in my periphery, I keep blinking, blinking, blinking,
until the white lines of my fist become soft, blurred.

From the Dining Table

We share a wooden board of marshmallows and paraffin.
We are adults having adult coffee and talking about health issues.
The easy armchairs almost send us horizontal in the nostalgic light
and now we are wary to trust our bodies to flat-pack upholstery.

The light bulb swings away from the blustering heater.
In my mind, you unravel its tight coils of copper to remember
the boy who stole a light bulb from the restaurant
who plucked it out of his pocket as we waited for the bus home.

A tiny blister formed on your index finger.
I watch you press it against the cool glass of the jug.
I watch you swirl it through melted ice water.
I watch you conduct the orchestra crackling over the radio.

The biscuit crumbles and the marshmallow strings from your lips.
We check the film times at no less than three picture houses.
There are rumours of snow and the streetlights have come on.
It is only four and everything feels like beginning.

Fangirl

Cinnamon Honey Butter

Popcorn spits and oil sputters from the open pan,
onto the stairwell and into the hands of a boy
who, eyebrows high and jaw slack, laughs
and throws it, catching it tightly between his teeth.
Not seasoned with the cinnamon honey butter,
but salted, it melts by the warmth of his tongue.
Ahead, the beekeepers are making a commotion.
Glass shards have fallen between the cobblestones.
A grandmother curses her husband's unreliable hands.
Locals begin tallying pathways in the sky.
The boy turns and translates for the tourists:
the stars are out and so are the bees – run!

The Spring I Decided I Needed a Sugar Daddy

In what was not a surprising turn of events,
it became necessary to invite myself to the Met Gala.
I experienced a cheap thrill in telling people I was flying
to New York to gatecrash their gated party.
I fought a quiet, pulsing rage that there were more people
reading true crime in the airport, than in either
of the two libraries I worked in to research
the etymology of sugar daddy. After which,
I understood that I needed to find an adoring door-mat type
who would be sometimes surprised in love nests.
After which, I disregarded the idea of love nests.
These fools in flip-flops could not understand
that in order to write properly about missing something
I needed to be there in person to miss it.
Or, how else would I know the close betrayal
of fame and fortune and a couple of unreleased sex tapes?

Slow-Shutter

Somewhere in the city there are sirens.
Cameras click click like cicadas.
The driver looks in his rear-view mirror
to find the boy in the back of the taxi crying.

The clubs are busy and people don't care
if the drugs and alcohol are overpriced,
if they understand the emotional complexity of noise,
if they'll remember to water their urban planters.

The driver wants to say something serious.
The driver reaches for the volume control.
The boy recognizes CHAMPAGNE SUPERNOVA.
The boy uncurls to fasten his seatbelt.

You and I, we live and die.

Oh No!

At their flagship store, the New York virgin made her first purchase
from Victoria's Secret, where she was thrilled to find the
    semi-annual sale
and a bra from their **very sexy** collection that was actually quite
    comfortable.
She spent so long searching for seamless silk, and due to the
    anti-socialness
of umbrellas, there was now an unavoidable thunderstorm in
    Times Square.

The pink and black paper bag disintegrates under her fingertips,
the tissue paper melts, the underwear falls into the first puddle
with a gentle splosh, her heart sinks. She shouts *oh no!*
A kind person stops but they know it is impossible to simulate sex
    appeal in soggy lace.
She walks into Olive Garden with knickers in her pockets and
    three bralettes
stuffed under her cardigan. She never feels **very sexy** in them
but thinks of her Nan, and when she told her, how hard she
    laughed.

Breakdown

It had taken more than six hours
and three text messages to Ethiopia

to set up the Arts Council-funded turntable
I needed to accurately audio describe

the artwork of the strawberry-milk pink,
coke-bottle green records,

only to find it wasn't a broken cable,
but a loose connection on the inside:

two metal prongs too far apart
to talk to each other properly,

one that didn't even know the other
was there trying to hear it.

There was something serendipitous
about being heartbroken during the release

of a heartbreak album, with the postman
already tired of square sleeve parcels

and the neighbours already sick of hearing
heartbreaker's twelve songs on repeat.

Exhibitionist

The inside guy is taking his time. This isn't a museum of tripwires and pressure sensors. This is a seven-camera situation with a security guard calculating the cost of a tutu for his twin daughter's birthday. Three nights' work, only drinking instant coffee brought from home and steak bakes from the shop further away. A no-brainer.

A twang of bass catches his attention. Pushing headphones further into his ears, he restarts the song then pushes the repeat button. The mood has been set. He snakes his head to THE CHAIN as he strolls through the room of contemporary portraits. He finds one he likes, pushes his nose close enough to the canvas to smell the acrylic, and looks over the brush strokes. It's alright. A little heavy-handed.

The gift shop is the most heavily guarded room in the building. Local jewellery in tight glass cabinets, metal shutters pulled down over the branded hoodies, scarves, and umbrellas. There is no cash in the till to be taken. Only the stationery is left unattended. The pencils pre-sharpened and glowing metallic green under the emergency lighting. He runs the graphite over his fingertip to gauge its softness. It smudges just how he wanted.

Back under the blind spot of the camera, he scans for a wall without art. He has two choices: one with crumbling cream paint, the other underneath the staircase but not weathered by direct sunlight. He can't hear the scratch of the pencil, only feel the pulse of the song. He makes mercurial movements, balances the shading well, and signs his debut in the museum sector sloppily bottom right. He doesn't need to glance at his watch so takes a moment to stand back and read:

DAMN YOUR LOVE. DAMN YOUR LIES.
THE BEST HEISTS HAPPEN AT NIGHT.

Cat Rave, Kitten Disco

On a Friday night, we get the bus to Portadown,
to an art gallery that we've never been to.
On the bus full of people with local accents,
we only know two. The first: the artist who taught
me to code in a converted science lab, who talked
to me about taxes and laser safety training courses.
The second: a brief date I wouldn't recognize again.
The gallery is showing a mobile interactive laser sculpture
for cats. There are printed kittens on vinyl on the walls.
Catnip periodically disperses from the glitter ball
next to the GoPro. We watch embedded blue-tit videos.
We dance as rave music thrums from the speakers.
In a room for dog-people only, a game of table tennis begins.
As we stand in front of a wall of nine televisions waiting
for cats to catch the lasers, we are photographed by a professional.
It is only when a friend shows me a photo of a cat that wasn't his
that I realize my face blindness extends to kittens.

Brass and Pearl

The showman was head down and full of hay fever
when he heard about the man whose wife played cello

who sometimes had a cello full of honeycomb and bees
who sometimes played the cello full of honeycomb and bees

because she liked the way the vibration changed
and everybody knows the bees are disappearing

but not that there aren't enough hollow trees
left here for them to find their own homes.

The showman smiled only to himself
when he caught in the periphery of the shop window

a revelation both perfect and incomplete:
a gold honeybee earring with a glass drop pearl.

The Crowd Are Young and Full of Tears and Snot and Sweat

Future writers / future teachers / future fathers / future dreamers /
future bankers / future cleaners / future mothers / future leaders /

He signed some t-shirts for a couple pre-show
whose future doesn't stretch as far as his own.

Future preachers / future healers / future readers / future speakers /
future schemers / future planners / future brokers / future seekers

Magnificent Desolation + Moon Songs

It has been fifty years since the first man walked
across the surface of the moon, so the radio is playing

the entirety of *The Dark Side of the Moon*
(Remastered) to celebrate the occasion.

We speak about the moon differently
now that we have translated Curiosity from Mars.

We write about the moon differently
now that we know we littered there too,

and I think it's going to be a long, long time
before we forgive ourselves.

Outbid

I understand the market of pop star merchandise beautifully.
I completed my jumper collection with an import:
a North American Tour exclusive in bright washout yellow.
The seller would not post internationally but I have memorized
my American housemate's American address for this reason.

On the resale market, I find the things most undervalued:
a very early *Live at the Troubadour* t-shirt from May 2017.
The seller is a cousin of the drummer so couldn't appreciate
it was the singer's first show with Stevie Nicks, couldn't know
the crowd cried as they performed LEATHER AND LACE in public.

Give Pop Music, Give Peace a Chance

A grandmother stands in the Terrace Hill Garden
as the foliage shifts and trembles in the wind.

Her grandchildren explore as fungi rise and retreat
along the beech tree bark on the woodland floor.

Her dog vaults over a stroll of bluebells,
and the grandmother is happy in the sunken garden

watching each contour, sketching the valley,
searching her sprawling city for home.

The Young Ranger, runs to help collect
the grass cuttings and the fallen plums,

points, and shouts at the Small Copper butterfly
landing on the short-blade scythe: *Look, a gorgeous thing!*

The grandmother, knowing this place is a gorgeous thing,
remembers perpetual rain clouds, pop music, potential,

Marmalade, Deep Joy, a telegram from John and Yoko,
the thrill of running coloured chalk through the ends of her hair.

She remembers sticking her thumb pad against the pin-back
of a badge that served as her first concert ticket.

She traces the loop and swirl of her fingertip,
finds ink smudges from felt-tip pens and placards for peace.

There are signs of the seasons turning.
Nothing small or insignificant is rooted here.

Ink and Hellebore

It is Thursday and Digital Detox Day in the Botanic Gardens.
I took a tour of the Tropical Ravine, where they let us
into the staff-only access areas to see the pineapple plants up close.
They weren't doing well overcrowded by big banana leaves.
Our tour guide asks if we have any questions and somebody asks
about the history of the vertical panes of glass, and if
the Belfast Botanical and Horticultural Society were still active
     today.
Then it is quiet, and we are about to move from the Palm House,
when I raise my hand and I say *yes, I have a question.*
I like your plant tattoos. Can you identify the species?
and nobody else is interested in our conversation so he says
thank you. Now that I've been here a while, I try to pick native plants.
and I think I could marry this guy but then he says
my girlfriend did them. I can give you her details and I say
yes, that is exactly why I was asking.

Rings

At the Electric Ballroom,
I dry my hair under cheap disco lights.
I watch the girl on the holographic
roller skates glide rings around me.

I only popped in because the popcorn
chicken and curly fries were half-off.
The sign said the floor was less sticky
than you would imagine it to be.

The girl salchows and swaps with
the geriatric cashier cracking gum.
I smirk; I surrender my gold credit card
and let her ring up my first pair of skates.

Stolen

I cannot talk about the fireworks of faint nausea,
the clouds of longing atoms or the toothache.
In the harbour of a yawn the knot of sorrow
comes undone. I pull it tight.
I was happy lying awake
when there came a sound,
the sorrow tenderly, tenderly,
hanging in the low snarl of midnight skies.
I had been warned of a motionless god,
his shining door shut and bolted.
Oh, a straight bright soul is not enough
but I begin to see it has done some good.
I never believed the best could be expected.
These mad mysterious days are warm.
Grief is a splendid thing to fear,
and I am ready to love and un-love.

Valley Road

I watched the opera in Vienna
then drove through the night
to meet him for breakfast in Italy.

The olive trees grew shadows
as he waited for my roadster
in silhouette ahead of the sun.

It hadn't been a slow winter.
He had tattoos I hadn't seen yet.
I had a scar from an unripe lemon.

I saw him first against the shutters
of the closed café with everything
exactly as I had expected it to be.

In the tremble of sunlight he held
cornettos wrapped in ribbons.
And absolutely new, his happiness.

Fanfic

The Boy Who

first time I see the boy in the borrowed jesus t-shirt
he's hiding in the bathroom of a house party
trying to forget that he kissed a girl just to impress his friends
he knows that I'm thinking *wow, what a cool t-shirt*
and he's weepy from the loud music and alcohol so he rests
the back of his head against the cool glass of the mirror and I
sit in the bathtub as he tells me about his housemate
who he met in a gay club that he definitely didn't know
was a gay club and who's in charge of sorting all the bills
and rent and has enough influence to declare their sofa
comfortable and free for as long as he needed it to be
whilst his mother was confused / sick and his father gone
and how he panicked when the housemate offered their open
overfilled wardrobe with brand-new-labels-still-on things
but relaxed when the housemate gave him the jesus t-shirt
because he had nothing and the housemate told him
take it this will look best with your blue eyes

Woozy

the boy who was drunk
on the late night and woozy
from the neon face paint
caught the eye of the boy
who had a butterfly tattoo

the boys didn't spare a second
thought for the waiting taxi
the boys cycled through the
city sprawled on a single bike
the boys were young and
foolish and very much alive

At the Electric Piano

in a different universe the boys met at the bus stop
avoiding eye contact with a pile of banana milk sick
the bus was too far away to be a comfortable wait
so the boy who transferred schools mid-year invited
the boy who he had never spoken to before home
then fought electrons of nervous energy when he said yes

when the needle dropped slowly onto the vinyl
heavy beats of dubstep pulsed from the record player
the boy who didn't know vinyl could sound that way
threw his head forward and crashed the tip of his teeth
against the green glass of his beer bottle to laugh

later when the conversation got a little personal
the boy who hid secrets sat easily at the electric piano
and played so tenderly that the room felt different
and it was possible things had changed between them

A Thousand Lives

the boy who lived a thousand lives in a single day
said something careless and everything stopped

silence   stretched   between   them

the boy who thinks they should take things slower
cannot return any text messages and evades sleep

belief   brings   them   back   together

Scrambled Eggs

the boys were tangled together under a winter duvet
snubbing the already bright sun to stare at the other
sleeping only to get caught mid-smile and pretend
themselves back to sleep so neither had to move

through the thin walls of the flatshare they heard
the metallic clang of scrambled eggs being stirred
a shout at the use of sea salt then the slow boil
of the kettle and its delicate steam climbing the walls

the boy who had another boy in his bed
for the first time rolled over and into the arms
of the other boy who was tired and trusting
and not at all tempted by the scrambled eggs

Mascara

the boy who didn't understand the power of his words
told his housemate that the shoes in the hallway weren't his
but belonged to the boy who he had a thing with
and that just because he liked another boy didn't mean
he was the same as the housemate or liked lavender mascara

the housemate sat with the boy who didn't understand pride
told him that there wasn't one single way to love and un-love
the most important thing was that he'd found someone he liked
the boys and girls who came before him had to fight and lie
they suffered and died and grieved and there was no dignity
so it was a very dangerous thing to put himself above people
who campaigned with courage and loss their whole lives
just because they liked glitter and were tired of being terrified

Swimming Pool

the boy who could've been great at water polo
with his long arms and excellent eyesight underwater
despite the hot chlorine air making his head swim
had been in bed with blankets pulled up to his ears
long enough that the shadow around him worried enough
that as he soothed the boy who was still breathing slowly
he was soft and gentle and lit quiet candles

until both boys remembered the hurt the worry the nausea
the fear the fear the fear the fear the fear the fear the fear
that everything overwhelming would ease eventually
and the swimming pool was heated throughout the year

Fan Mail

Ally

I subscribe
to a newsletter
from somebody
who writes better than I do
on boy bands,
on bodies,
on catching up and acting your age,
on housekeeping and closure,
on fine line,
on uncomplicated boys,
on getting it,
in profile.

Look, This Is How It Really Feels

Excuse me, sorry, hi.

We took a photograph,
no distance between the two of us,

a tangled moment I could not stop
from rupturing out-of-body,

magnified through the window
of a small café in North London.

I remember fragments, the shallow questions
that people ask a collective popular object.

Within five minutes, I knew
I loved the stranger in my head.

Wild Thoughts

I am clinging to a notebook
manufactured for slow hands.

In February, I was interviewed with friends
who shared the same sun sign as me,

as we slept on sidewalks and daydreamed
that we were well and rested.

I keep getting stuck skipping over words.
In a nightclub that I could legally get into,

with unwavering fondness,
I fall into crisis all over again.

I Promise to Not Be So Absent

Inside the back issues I find prayers
on housekeeping and remorse written
in rose-coloured permanent marker.
Adolescence is a wild beast.

Like the Washing Machine on Spin Cycle

I am blonde and drunk dancing in the dark
to nice boys with acoustic guitars.
I intended to be on my own
but it's fun to put on a good show
of awkward hip thrusts and hurt feet.
There is something that reminds me
of the best photo from a cheap camera.
The hue of sweetness and ease extends
to the endearing flat at the edge of town,
to the beautiful sexy pirate prince, who spins
soft-edged and boyish in a white t-shirt.

Ghost

He dances to layered vocals,
navigates the cool guy criticism
in private conversations and parlour games.

He translates adjectives into chord progressions
and to feel good he describes the sunflowers
in the kitchen: signs of swagger and joy.

He is afraid of the uproar
but is lucky enough to be beautiful.

In a Time When Joy Feels Like an Endangered Resource

Things are very simple –
    protect each other.

Profile

In the end, it is impossible to forget the beauty of abandoned
  pop stars.
There is a sense they withstood the first few punches in the
  media landscape,
and stitched together the things they loved with trademark
  enthusiasm.
Do not fear their dulcimers and sparkly oven stickers; their
  mushroom lunches;
their behind-the-scene meditations. Let them discover drunken
  karaoke –
let them defend the quiet hour of time they can ride around
  Malibu in a Tesla.

ハリー

You found something peculiar
being anonymous in Japan

even with the katakana of your name
embroidered onto soft hoodie fabric

you let the shiba inu lick the residential plants
hiding from the residential air-conditioning unit

you jogged the yellow-tiled steps
in yellow-striped socks

you pushed aside the painful stage
of growing out curls with gravity

in a place that seemed to stretch
sideways in all seasons

of all the moonstruck moments
this is the one I'd most like to meet.

Notes

These poems are perhaps best read while listening to the work of Harry Styles. The following notes are an excellent starting point in identifying the connections between my work and his.

The epigraph is quoted from Rob Sheffield's *Rolling Stone* interview, 'The Eternal Sunshine of Harry Styles'.

FANDOM:
Many of these poems take their titles from the tracklists of *Fine Line* and *Harry Styles* by Harry Styles. 'Sweet Creature' was collaged from Act 3, Scene 3 of *Othello* where the phrase 'sweet creature' originally appears.

FANFIC:
The Harry Styles song 'From the Dining Table' plays in season 1, episode 10 of *Druck*, the German remake of *Skam*. These poems were initially inspired by Isak and Even from *Skam*, created and written by Julie Andem.

FAN MAIL:
These poems were collaged from the following editions of Allyson Gross's newsletter *better than words*, 'a round-up of thinkpieces & essays on (former & forever) members of One Direction': #13 on bodies; #6 on catching up, and acting your age; #11 on housekeeping and closure; #12 on uncomplicated boys and Niall; #13 on fine line; #14 on getting it; #15 in profile.

These materials were always used following the Center for Media & Social Impact's Code of Best Practices in Fair Use for Poetry.

Acknowledgements

'Sweet Creature' was first published in *The Tangerine*. 'Meet Me in the Hallway' was first published in *The Stony Thursday Book*. 'Ever Since New York' and 'From the Dining Table' were first published in *The Open Ear*.

'Give Pop Music, Give Peace a Chance' was commissioned by The National Trust NI to commemorate fifty years since the Pop for Peace event at Minnowburn. 'Ink and Hellbore' was first published by *Poetry Birmingham Literary Journal*. 'Stolen' was first published by *The Poetry Jukebox*.

Earlier editions of 'At the Electric Piano' and 'A Thousand Lives' were first published in *Poetry Ireland Review*. 'Scrambled Eggs' and 'Swimming Pool' were first published in *Banshee*.

'/\ᑌ—' was first published as a British Sign Language digital arts installation co-created by Robin Price as part of Create:Innovate:Armagh's Digital Mentorship Award. 'Cat Rave, Kitten Disco' takes place at Robin's solo installation Feline Mobile Disco.

Thank you to Queen's University Belfast for the Sir Thomas Dixon Travel Scholarship that allowed me to visit *CAMP: Notes on Fashion* at The Met and write 'Oh No!', 'The Spring I Decided I Needed a Sugar Daddy' and 'Brass and Pearl'; and for the Santander Universities Cultural Exchange to the University of Petra, Jordan to inspire 'Cinnamon Honey Butter'.

Thank you to: Harry Styles Fashion Archive, United By Pop, and Treat Harry With Kindness Updates. Thank you to the *Another Man*, *Beauty Papers* and *Rolling Stone* photo shoots for their inspiration and bedroom wallpaper.

To: Harris Reed for the pirate prince look, Harry Lambert for the tour wardrobe, and Allyson Gross for all the newsletters. These resources made some details in these poems possible.

Thank you to Leontia Flynn, Stephen Sexton and Padraig Regan for their time on earlier editions of this work.

Thank you to Jessica Traynor for thoughtful edits and guidance.

Thank you to Laura Cassidy, Claire Hennessy and Eimear Ryan for making this publication process so enjoyable.

Thank you to everyone at the Seamus Heaney Centre (Queen's University Belfast) and the University of Exeter for their conversation, care, and collaboration over the years.

Thank you to the Arts Council of Northern Ireland National Lottery funds for the opportunity to explore my creative practice, and for the grant to support transcribing this work into Braille.

Thank you to my family. To my Nan and Grandad for always asking if I've written another poem. To my sister, for mistaking blah blah blah for a poem in which I was trying new things, and to my parents for reading the finished things.

Thank you to my friends of the newly formed Craft Night for allowing *Fine Line* to soundtrack our crafting adventures.

Thank you to Milena for everything in Belfast and everything beyond.

Thank you Harry, for the absolute joy of working on this.

BANSHEE
PRESS

Banshee Press was founded in 2014 by Laura Cassidy, Claire Hennessy and Eimear Ryan to publish exciting and contemporary new writing from Ireland and around the world. *Banshee* literary journal is published twice a year, in March and September.

The Banshee Press list launched in September 2019 with *Paris Syndrome*, the debut collection of stories by Lucy Sweeney Byrne. *Gold Light Shining* is the publisher's first poetry title.

WWW.BANSHEELIT.COM